Summer

by Alice Low

illustrated by Roy McKie

To Joe C. and Stephanie Kathryn
—A.L.

www.randomhouse.com/kids

ISBN: 0-375-81235-0 (trade)   0-375-91235-5 (lib. bdg.)
Library of Congress Catalog Card Number: 63-15628

Printed in the United States of America   May 2001   10 9 8 7 6 5 4 3

BEGINNER BOOKS®

A Division of Random House, Inc.

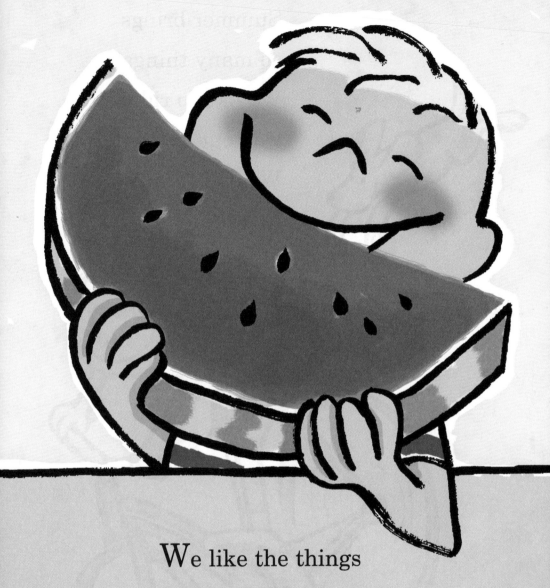

We like the things
that summer brings.
It brings the sun.
It brings the heat.
It brings the things
we like to eat.

Summer brings
so many things!
We like to ride
way out of town.
We like to ride
uphill and down.

It feels so good
when we go fast.
We like to feel
the breeze go past.

We ride and ride
about a mile,
and then we stop
and eat a while.
We like cold things.
We eat them up.
And when we eat,
so does our pup.

We like the things
that summer brings.
It brings us fireworks
late at night,
all red and yellow,
blue and white.
They go up high.
They are such fun!
Look! Look!
There goes another one.

Some summer days
we take a ride.
The car gets very
hot inside.
And when we sit
in all that heat,
we wish that we
had used our feet.

At last we are
no longer hot.
Cold water cools us
off a lot.
It cools us off
down to our toes.
Our pup is going
to cool his nose.

Summer brings
so many things.
Summer brings us
rides on swings!

We swing up high
into the trees.
We swing so fast
we make a breeze.

Then down we go
into some hay.
We like to play
this game all day.

Summer brings us things with wings!

We like to catch them

with a net

and see how many

we can get.

In summertime
we say hello
to all the fish
way down below.

They look at us.
They seem to say,
"What kind of fish
have come our way?"

A summer fair!
A fair is fun!
In summertime
we go to one.
Around, around,
around we go.
The ground is very
far below.

Summer sun
brings garden fun.

We have to water well,
we know,
to make our garden
grow and grow.

You water me.
I water you.
And that will make us
grow fast, too!

Some summer nights
we cook and eat.
Our pup is not
so very neat.

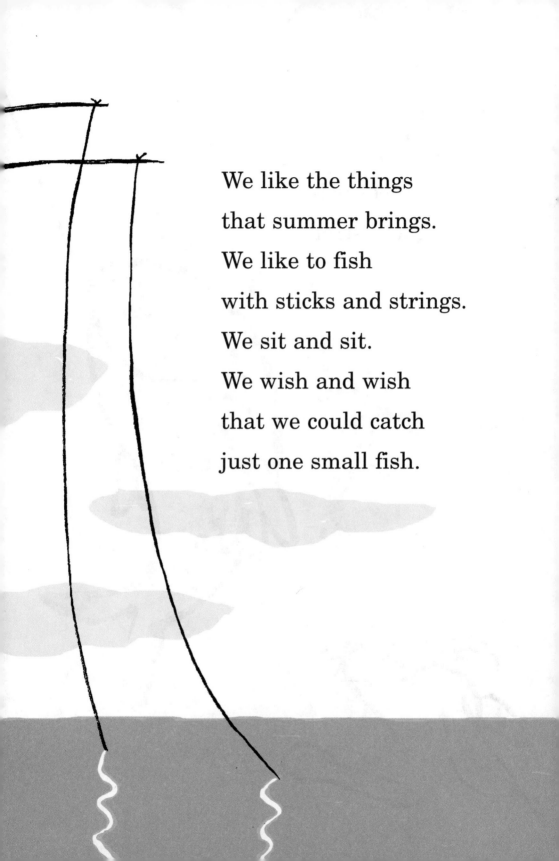

We like the things
that summer brings.
We like to fish
with sticks and strings.
We sit and sit.
We wish and wish
that we could catch
just one small fish.

Some days we catch one
ten feet long.
And ten-feet fish
are big and strong.

They get away!
They take our hook.
We never take them
home to cook.

We like this way
to spend a day.
We make a sand house
on the shore.
We make some windows
and a door.

Then waves come up.

They come up fast.

Sometimes our sand house

does not last.

But there is lots

of sand to dig

to make another

just as big.

When we go out
on summer nights,
we see the fireflies
with their lights.

We catch them.
They will give us light
to find our way
back home at night.

We ask a farmer,
"Will you stop
and let us ride
back home on top?"

We let the fireflies go away.

The moon is out.

It lights our way.

We hear the horse

go clop-clop-clop.

Our pup goes

fast asleep on top.

We stay awake
and think of things . . .
the happy things
that summer brings!